How to draw Steampunk

Creating Stunning steampunk pictures

by Amy Hughes

Table of Contents

Disclaimer

While all attempts have been made to verify the information provided in this book, the author does assume any responsibility for errors, omissions, or contrary interpretations of the subject matter contained within. **The information provided in this book is for educational and entertainment purposes only. The reader is responsible for his or her own actions and the author does not accept any responsibilities for any liabilities or damages, real or perceived, resulting from the use of this information.**

The trademarks that are used are without any consent, and the publication of the trademark is without permission or backing by the trademark owner. All trademarks and brands within this book are for clarifying purposes only and are the owned by the owners themselves, not affiliated with this document.

Introduction

They are impacted by steampunk in their music, as well as in their attire, outline of their instruments, and even the anecdotal personas that they convey with them in front of an audience. Beside steampunk rock, there is rap and hip-bounce music affected by steampunk, and as a rule incorporates a profound however up-beat bass and verses that either delineate the life of a frantic researcher, or a post-prophetically catastrophic world.

Steampunk has been gotten by the craftsmanship culture shockingly quick. You can without much of a stretch discover artistic creations of airships and other flying machines crossing dark skies above tremendous, forlorn scenes. Such craftsmanship can be discovered on the web, at your nearby workmanship shows, and in displays. While the reason and point of view of such artworks is dissimilar to whatever else, the workmanship styles can be fundamentally the same to different styles you have seen. While being dull and dismal, the fine art frequently portrays a vicious ocean, a prison like-lab, or a deadlock world, infrequently Frankenstein-esque. It is anything but difficult to bring up anything steampunk motivated in light of the fact that the style is especially one of a kind contrasted with others.

Attempting to disclose steampunk to some person that has never known about it is extremely troublesome. You may have heard this term now and again and still have no clue what they are alluding to. All things considered, now is your opportunity to learn everything about steampunk that you ever needed to know. Steampunk is a style of cosplay in which the cosplayers dress and talk in certain conduct. To put it plainly, steampunk alludes to a particular type of verifiable fiction.

Regularly steampunk takes a post-whole-world destroying setting in the Victorian period with substantial topics of steam-fueled apparatus. That is a decent general perspective of steampunk, however it can get a considerable measure more included. There are even diverse subgenres of the steampunk cosplay. Steampunk can take the type of Medieval Steampunk, Victorian Era Steampunk, Western Steampunk and that's only the tip of the iceberg!

Today steampunk has discovered its way into pretty much everything. After the film promotion of steampunk we additionally began to see a goad of steampunk realistic books. We even began seeing computer games get the reason. Prominent diversions like "Bioshock" are ridden with steampunk subjects. An enormous number of experts have begun building steampunk themed props. These carport mechanics have transformed pretty much all that we utilize and love into a steampunk thrill.

Genuine steampunk devotees regularly toss meet-ups. This is the place you break out each bit of complex steampunk clothing you possess, even your steampunk sleeve fasteners. You additionally need to catch up on your mid-century language. Dressing the part is one thing, however talking the discussion is an entire other monster. In the event that you have room schedule-wise to dedicate to taking in the language you can have some incredible times. The main downpoint to this way of life is the expense. Most things steampunk don't accompany shoddy stickers. You need to remember basically all that you are purchasing is 100% carefully assembled and unique, so the costs mirror this.

Chapter 1 – 1st picture

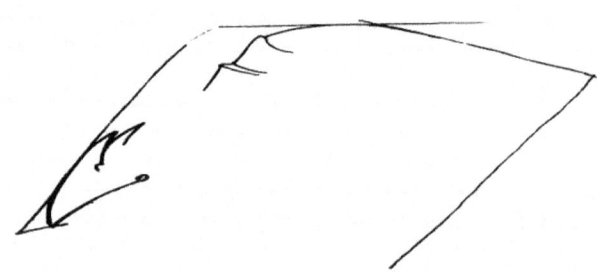

Step 1: Draw a few lines as the outlining of the drawing you will be making. And start with basic steps of sketching where you think the figures would start from.

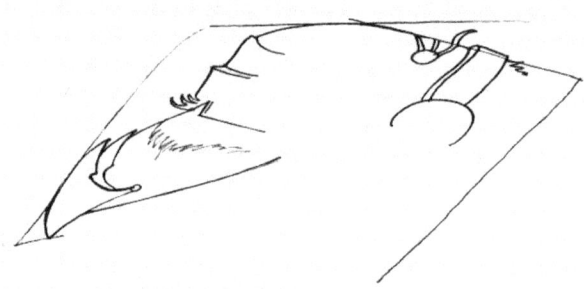

Step 2: After the basic outlining we can start giving the drawing basic lines and curves so that we can complete the figure. Make sure that the figure is inside the outlined area.

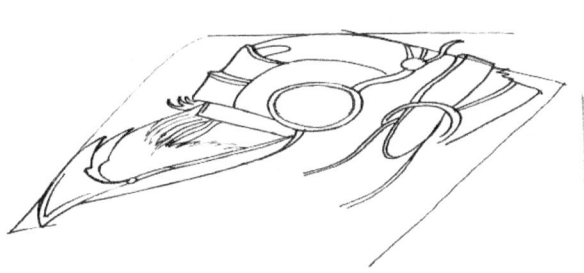

Step 3: Now we can see that the figure above shows something but we are not really sure what it is. It's a steampunk, so we have added and sketched the parts which were necessary.

Keep in mind the fundamental shapes and configuration of the parts above (most everything is round and hollow fit as a fiddle). Surf up every part above, and gather pictures of segments, and additionally old steam trains & vehicles for reference. When you are acquainted with the parts, you can then free outline voluntarily, however dependably utilize the references to keep it bona fide and acceptable.

Clench hand, concoct thoughts. Arrangement out what you need it to be, a biped robot? an auto? a tank? a multi legged strolling machine? Don't under evaluation "character". Add some identity or character to you machines, regardless of the possibility that it is soulless. The #1 objective ought to be an all around composed, adjusted, and eye getting machine. Stress over how it functions after you have some harsh portrays and states of something convincing, else it's not justified regardless of the exertion. I can't push this point enough.

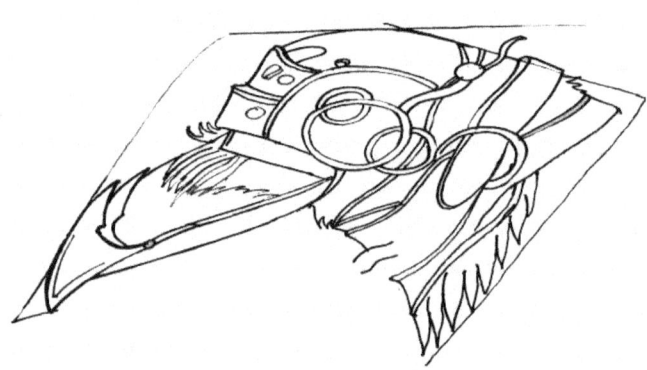

Step 4: Work free to begin with, regardless of the possibility that you choose the completion venture will be point by point and all around rendered. I more often than not lean toward the free and sluggish way, simply flounder it down and call it great, the length of you get the inclination and thought over, you don't generally need to deliberately draw out every teeth of an apparatus - the human personality is decent at associating and understanding only two or three lines. Be that as it may, you can go as subtle element as you like, it is just a complex decision.

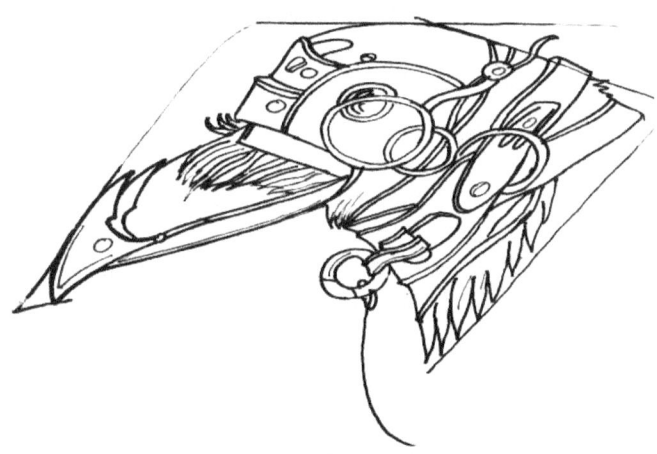

Step 5: As now you can see the steampunk looks like it, and we have added many parts and drawn the steampunk as it looks like.

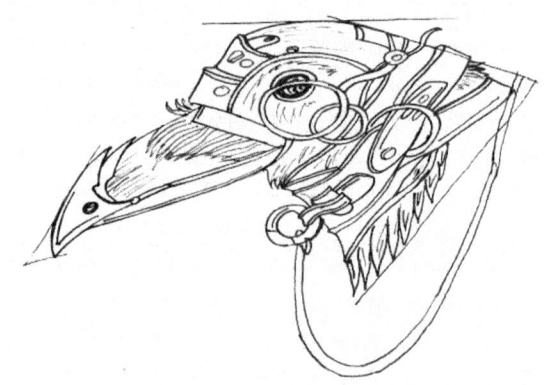

Step 6: Now the steampunk is completed with the finishing as well. Now we can erase the lines we drew in the 1st step and complete the steampunk by shading the inner parts of it.

Chapter 2 – 2ⁿᵈ picture

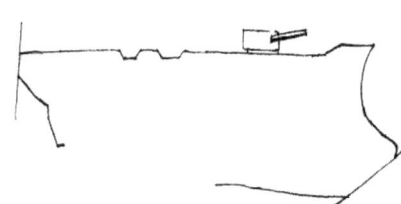

Step 1: So when the normal worldwide temperature goes up a couple of degrees, it will alarm humankind into embracing nursery gas confinements and so forth to back off out of the emergency.

Isn't that so?

Potentially. In any case, there's a banality about "the best of goals" that very well might apply. Unfortunately, there's something called positive criticism. Western Siberia, as an illustration, has seen a 3° Celsius temperature rise—and covered under softening permafrost is a peat swamp bigger than France and Germany joined. That permafrost—set up subsequent to the last ice age— started to soften a couple of years back and will conceivably twofold the measure of methane in our environment.

What's more, western Siberia is not the only one; there are comparative clathrates—caught methane takes—everywhere throughout the earth. 251 million years back these pockets emitted into the air, also, almost every type of life on Earth was wiped out, for 20 million years.

It is very conceivable we have under 10 years to everything except stop the human expansion of nursery gasses in the event that we are to avert runaway an unnatural weather change.

Probability: many individuals will let you know a ton of things, for a parcel of diverse political purposes, yet in any event a few of us here at SteamPunk are about deadened with trepidation. Survival: Survival, in the event that it can be called a wonder such as this, may just be found in underground, self-managing settlements. We recommend you pack a book to peruse, since you will be underground for more than humankind has already.

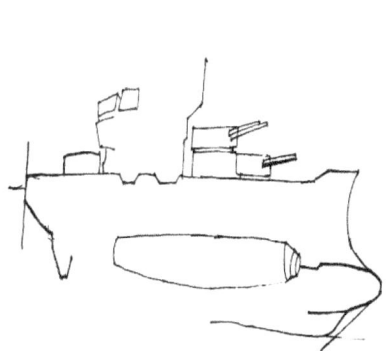

Step 2: We can make the outlining of this skip which is being drawn. So that later in the steps we can sketch the parts and turn this half figure complete.

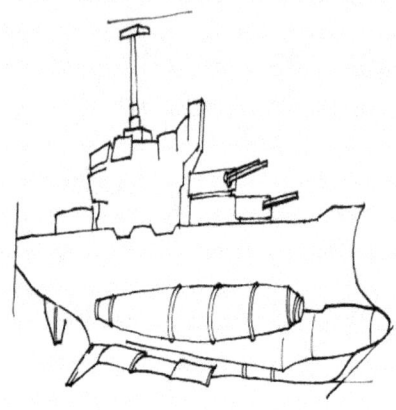

Step 3: Now in this step we can complete the ship by joining the lines and sketching few parts and by using parallel lines as you can see in the cylinder.

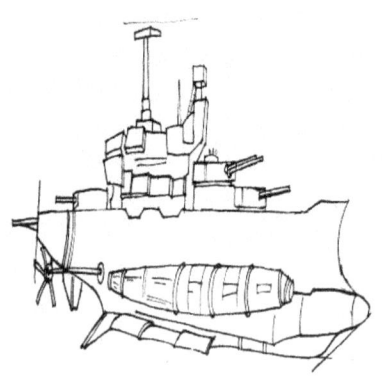

Step 4: Now we can complete the ship by making other parts of it as you can see in the figure above.

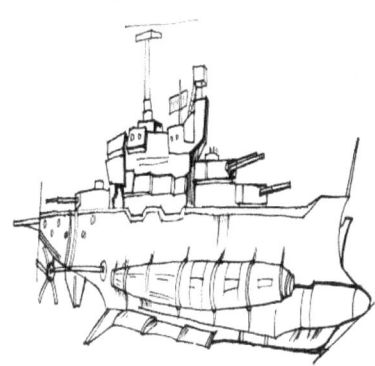

Step 5: Now our ship is ready we can sketch the parts of the boat by using different types of sketching.

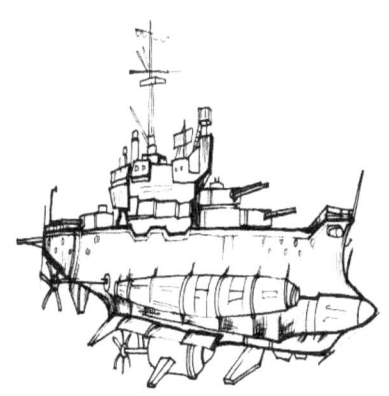

Step 6: In the final step we can use better shading techniques to give the final figure the best look.

Chapter 3 – 3ʳᵈ Picture

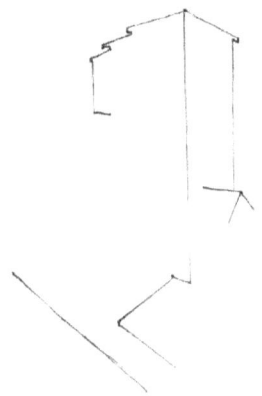

Step 1: We have started this image by making few lines to show the building.

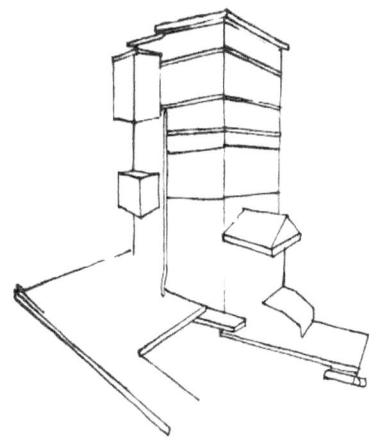

Step 2: Here in this image we have added a few lines to the step 1 and showed a proper building, later in other few steps we will cover all the things which are needed in order to complete this building.

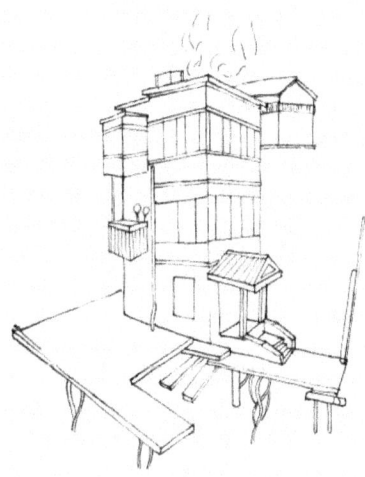

Step 3: Here in this step we have completed the basic things which were needed in order to show the complete building and the houses on the backside.

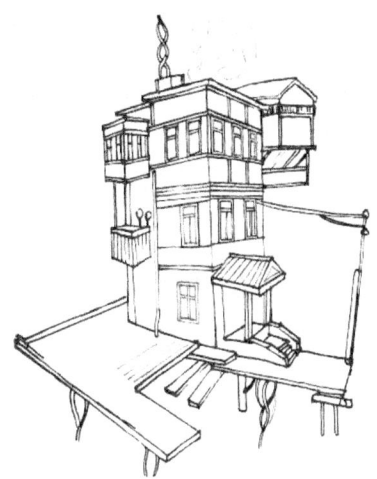

Step 4: In this step we have worked on the shading part of this building so that it looks complete and we can figure out where the balconies are, where the windows are. And the road which is on the backside of the building and the houses on the backside. Now as we can see the building looks complete.

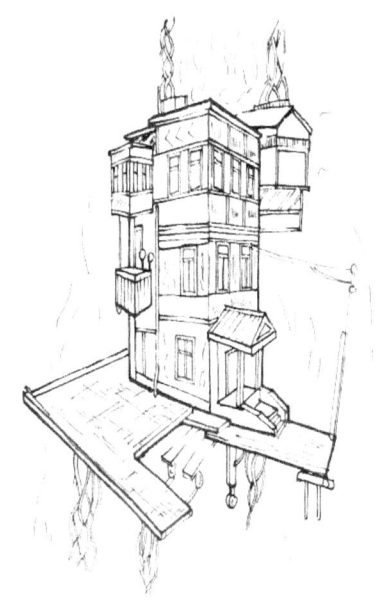

Step 5: Now the work is completed as we can see we have the final sketch of the building and with that we can see the chimneys which are above the building and the house on the backside. We can also see a way.

Chapter 4 – 4th picture

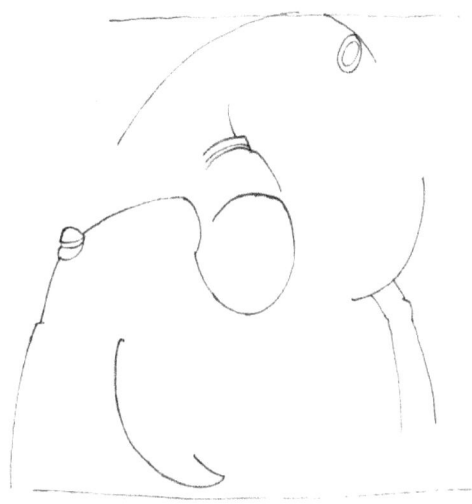

Step 1: At that point choose where to lay out the engine(s). Motors can be at any point, they work fine and dandy anyway they are situated. Lay out a few apparatuses or sprocket/chains that will be noticeable. The cylinders must power specifically to the principle drive shaft, or adapted to it. The most straightforward is to simply make the cylinder shaft in the same bearing as the drive shaft, then again, you can course it anyway you need utilizing inclined apparatuses.

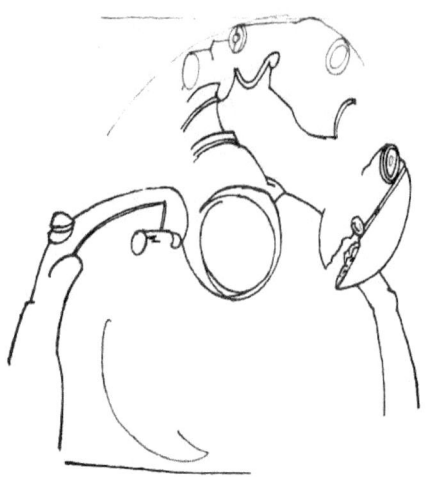

Step 2: Work out the locomotion.... in the event that you get befuddled about how something functions you can cover it up with body work. On the other hand, I think the convincing piece of steampunk is in how transparent things are, so I like demonstrating the greater part of the systems however much as could be expected.

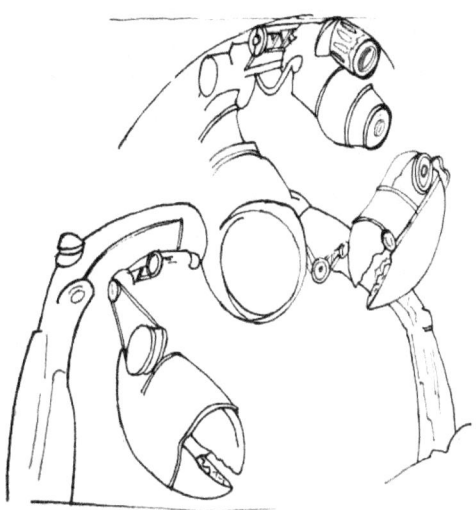

Step 3: Outline out the body work, attempt to keep the old tech feel. Right now you can conceal any mechanical subtle element that you can't, or are excessively apathetic, making it impossible to make sense of :)

Set down fundamental shading or shading, working out shapes and characterize planes & edges as you go

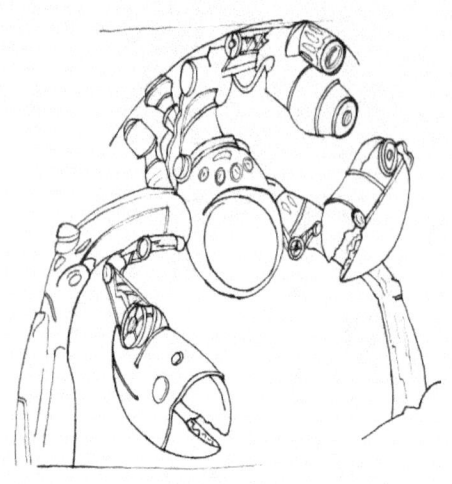

Step 4: Include solid shadow and shading.

Include articulations, for example, Victorian roused parchment work, bolts and so on. And in addition add point of interest with valves, levers and so on.

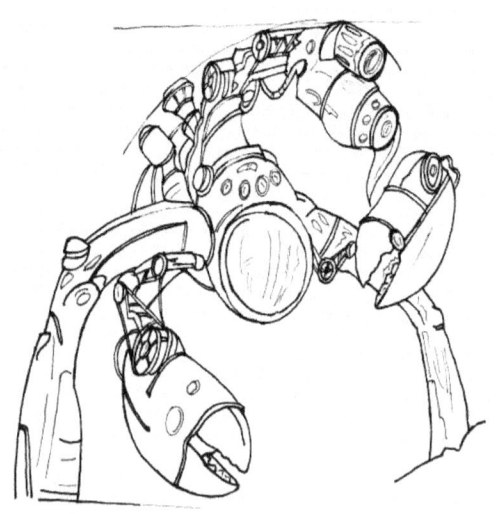

Step 5: On the off chance that you choose to include shading, you can add more and more shading to the parts of the figure. They regularly are dark, however not generally. Complements in metal, copper, or gold, and also shades of maroon, dim green, or blue.

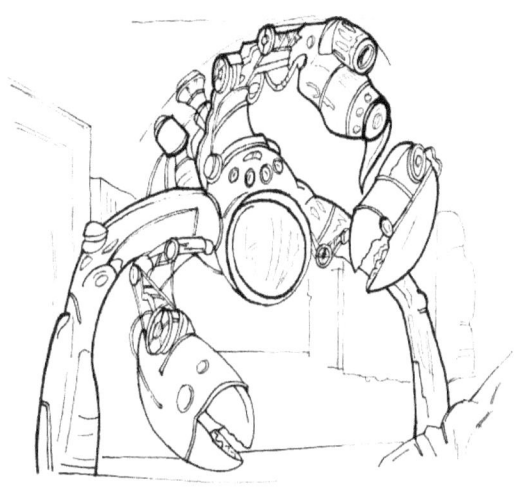

Step 6: Now you can see with the best shading we have done, the figure looks like the final drawing and the outcome of the steps followed above.

Chapter 5 – 5th Picture

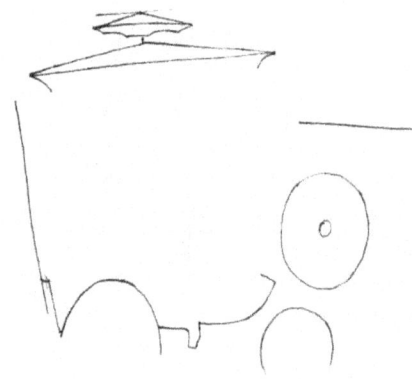

Step 1: we can start off by giving the image a pattern of a horse ride, how it is drawn. And the basic steps to complete it.

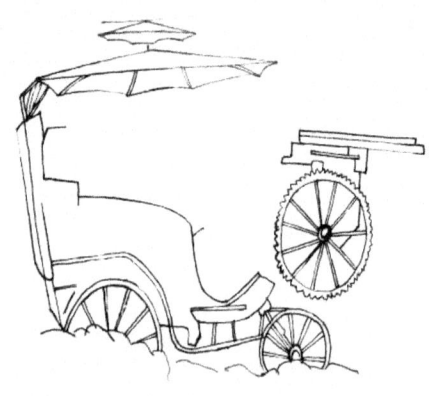

Step 2: Now in this step we are covering the shadow of the ride, as well as the tires of the ride.

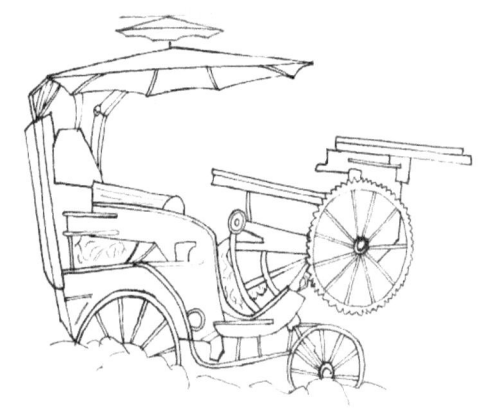

Step 3:

In this step we have completed the ride and given the proper outlines in order for it to look the best.

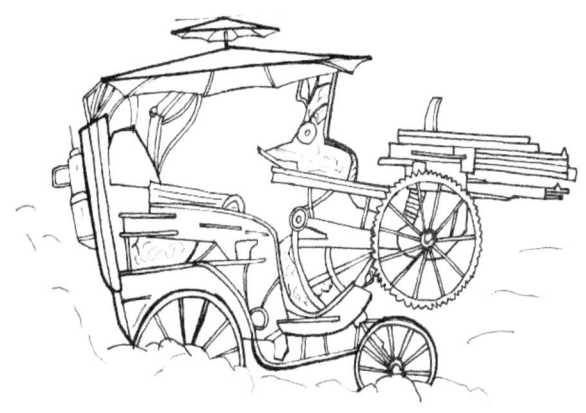

Step 4: With this step we are completed the figure as you can see in the image.

Conclusion

STEAMPUNK LITERATURE

This is the place it began. From exchange histories set in the Victorian period with steam innovation and here and there enchantment to time travel, privateers, and the sky is the limit from there, steampunk books, stories, funnies, and the movies, recreations, music, what's more, other social expressions they rouse envision full fledged pasts that never were, and that would have offered ascent to an altogether different present.

Steampunk workmanship & outline realizes the nonexistent questions, styles, and innovation of envisioned steampunk universes, in light of a common tasteful of materials, hues, subjects, shapes, themes, and style. With a do-it-without anyone's help state of mind also, accentuation on individual elucidation, the steampunk tasteful shows in each sort of craftsmanship and configuration, including style, furniture, also, devices and in addition the expressive arts. Steampunk creators/craftsmen/tinkerers make and bodge together the old and the new in inventive, shrewd, and lovely ways.

You may have heard this inquisitive expression bandied about in the media as of late, alongside pictures of individuals wearing Victorian garments and outfits, donning all way of surprising frill. You may have pondered internally what the deuce is this?

The term Steampunk started in the 1980's and is utilized to depict a subculture of Science Fiction and Fantasy with an accentuation on option history.

The universes of Steampunk normally concentrate on the period generally known as the Victorian Era with numerous stories set in Britain and America, in spite of the fact that there are various International Adventures and a huge Steampunk following in Japan. Since a large portion of these experiences include all way of peculiar, unordinary and out of date methods of transport, these stories can occur anyplace above, beneath or even inside the world!

In spite of the fact that the term Steampunk has been credited to the Author K. W. Jeter when authoring an expression for the books of Tim Powers and James Blaylock, you can locate its initial impacts in progress of HG Wells and Jules Verne. The Time Machine and 20,000 Leagues under the Sea could surely be seen as exceedingly persuasive works and references for future creators.

Steampunk isn't reflected in any one structure, there are books, realistic books, Jewelry, Fashion, activities and garments. You can frequently discover Steampunk impacts crawling into numerous works of art, and computer games and Role Playing Games.

There are a colossal number of sites devoted to this energizing class, with new locales and fan pages seeming every day. There are likewise various shops which convey a scope of all way of items including Steampunk Jewelry, Quill Pens, USB Drives and Goggles.

Since Steampunk is a genuinely free term, individuals make all way of enrapturing understandings, without a doubt Steampunk can regularly be both an interesting, imaginative and entirely unconventional type.

As of late, the universe of Steampunk has been inching into the standard, through groups like Abney Park, computer games and TV arrangement.

A vast Steampunk affected up and coming discharge is Bioshock Infinity which is a videogame set to ship in 2012. The amusement happens in a city over the mists and conveys numerous unmistakable Steampunk and Dieselpunk impacts.

There are a wide range of translations of the term Steampunk, with diverse individuals contending what falls under this umbrella. Then again, it does appear to be clear that Steampunk was initially begat in the 1980's to characterize a particular sort of writing that was beforehand indistinct. This writing is typically set in, however not bound to, the Victorian time, and combined with advanced developments that may have been imagined amid this time.

Despite the fact that the term Steampunk wasn't begat until the 1980s, its inceptions can be followed back to the nineteenth century with sci-fi sentiment combined books by Jules Verne and H.G Wells. Jules Verne was not just persuasive through his books; Karel Zeman's film The Fabulous World of Jule Verne was exceptionally compelling, similar to Disney's adjustment of Verne's novel Twenty Thousand Leagues Under The Sea. The first TV Series of The Wild West in the 60s was outwardly all that much of the Steampunk classification. Steampunk appears to recommend "What may have been", had our advances in innovation been different;mechanical and steam fueled, maybe without the development of power. Therefore, the symbolism of Steampunk is constantly extremely cutting edge yet at the same time holds the Victorian style - envision metal, wood, glass and a lot of itemizing.

Steampunk itself is not constrained to writing. It has turned into a complete sub society, with Steampunk design, craftsmanship, amusements and even music. What with the fantastical symbolism utilized as a part of Steampunk books, it wouldn't have been long until individuals began to make devices and systems in this style. Individuals have now "steampunked" everything; from telephones to autos, PCs to try and houses! Steampunk dressing itself may not be the most conventional Victorian dress, but rather adds a fun turn to it, utilizing cutting edge and mechanical extras, to make an intriguing and inventive look.

In the most recent couple of years, Steampunk has turned out to be more powerful in standard society. Television Programs, for example, Doctor Who and Warehouse 13 both component Steampunk motivated things, the last having articles planned by Steampunk Artisan Richard Nagy. Justin Bieber even as of late had a feature highlighting metal systems and Steampunk outfits! Steampunk hasn't neglected to impact the regularly developing realistic novel culture either.

Artistic works of mid twentieth Century, and notwithstanding dating to the Victorian period, have affected the class known as Steampunk. While it is for the most part an artistic classification, it is likewise characterized by innovation, for example, steam motors that were fused into the period's sci-fi and dream. It's been depicted as a kind of Victorian-modern, however with more caprice and less vagrants or, as Jess Nevins said, "Steampunk is the thing that happens when Goths find cocoa."

Steampunk has discovered its way into different classifications, for example, sentiment, erotica, and youthful grown-up fiction. Likewise developing in prevalence are Steampunk garments, a line characterized by the unpleasant innovation of the mid 1900's the place a couple of goggles would fit in pleasantly. This individual style incorporates both apparel and gems and, while the garments are not precisely Victorian, including mechanical bits or insights of an a larger number of daring life than a normal Victorian native.

While the class incorporates the Victorian time, it incorporates propelled machines in light of nineteenth century innovation, and in addition the otherworldly also and may even happen in a different universe.

Obviously, Steampunk contraptions are coming into this present reality. Individuals have Steampunk'd everything from PCs, work areas, phone, watches and guitars to autos, cruisers, and homes. These items can shift from a grungy look of an overlooked obsolescent to the sparkly exhausted novelty of a Victorian refined man's club. These are metal and copper, glass and finished wood, imprinting and carving, and points of interest for the purpose of subtle elements.

At long last, Steampunk demonstrates a philosophical point too, which is to some degree a blend between the goals of imagination and confidence and the Victorian hopeful perspective without bounds. This last part has prompted allegations that Steampunk incorporates a decent lot of realm love, which is a sensible concern. Another feedback has been that Steampunk concentrates on the best of the past and discreetly clears the issues of the day under the mat.

Steampunk is a sub-classification of punk that is communicated in particular areas, for example, ensemble faires, renaissance faires, Blizzcon, Comic-Con, Halloween, the smoldering man celebration, vast festivals or maybe in a more personal setting with a gathering of companions, on a day outside over a cookout. It is not normally viewed as ordinary apparel, worn on a trek to the shopping center in light of the fact that the vast majority are new to the idea, and it is less an announcement against particular advanced social patterns, as a declaration of a thought of how things could be totally distinctive.

The Steampunk sort is based around the thought of the continuation of innovation along the confinements of steam force, as though the utilization of fossil fills, and different types of force had never been found. Copper tubing and metal metalwork are viewed as the components most used to develop devices and thingamajigs inside of these impediments. Blown glass and little measures of power can likewise be vital components in making "fiendish gadgets".

Steampunk attire and design is dated around the age where Steampower was most pervasive, so Victorian and Edwardian subjects are a staple when assembling an ensemble

The Steampunk class is dependably generally used to infer an envisioned future where we have come back to steam power because of the consumption of different assets. This thought takes into account low-innovative conceivable outcomes, and is in a few ways more great since it can join cutting edge dream. A couple of steampowered individual wings. Goliath ocean bearing vessels fit as a fiddle of an octopus.

In this manner, "Steampunk" could suggest somebody in today's reality who favors the thought of this other innovation existing over our present situation. Be that as it may, an ensemble can likewise be themed in an advanced sense, delineating an ordinary person who exists in reality as we know it where steam is the most utilized type of force. A charcoal besmudged urchin who lives up to expectations throughout the day in a production line giving steam energy to deliver wonders of advanced steam innovation. An abundance seeker who's weapons are formed from the leftovers of tore separated weapons of war, no more of utilization due to the lack of "old world fossil energizes, however refashioned to store a payload of steam weight with the end goal of dispatching a shot towards anything.

Sketching Drawing - The 3 fundamental contrasts

1. Sketching is generally looser and more liberated

At the point when individuals sketch it is more often than not to deliver a fast interpretation of a scene. This is regularly done in light of the fact that the scene isn't static, for example, a bistro scene with individuals traveling every which way. This kind of liquid, always showing signs of change circumstance, fits a quick way to deal with drawing we allude to as sketching. In this kind of sketching the goal is to get on paper the primary structures and lines of the scene. These lines and structures are regularly straightforward yet lovely in their extremely effortlessness. This type of fast drawing is likened to immaculate observation drawing and obliges a gifted eye and a snappy translation of the smoothness of the evolving scene.

The "detachment" of the lines in such portrays and the virtue of line and structure that gifted craftsmen can accomplish regularly ingrains an incredible vitality into the completed piece.

2. Sketching utilized for reference

Numerous specialists utilize fast portrays to investigate the different qualities and types of a scene for later use as reference material for a more inside and out drawing or painting. These speedy portrayals can be as straightforward or as nitty gritty as the craftsman requires however they are normally not thought to be done pieces in their own privilege; albeit once a craftsman has been made "popular" such outlines regularly get to be profitable. Representation books are a prominent strategy for gathering these sorts of reference portrayals.

3. Drawings and points of interest

A drawing is normally thought to be to a greater extent a completed piece than a portrayal. This by and large implies that a drawing will contain more visual data by method for point of interest and tonal interpretation than a representation. In any case, this is the place the line frequently gets to be obscured; when does a representation turn into a drawing?

Drawings are additionally normally finish articulations of a scene or subject contrasted with the short lived nature of numerous portrayals. Since drawings of liquid scenes, for example, the bistro situation already specified, are not by any stretch of the imagination down to earth the last drawing of such a scene will frequently be done far from the scene i.e. back at the craftsmen studio, utilizing portrayals as reference.

The meaning of a drawing most likely does not mean they are finished with a ruler! Certainly, absolutely structural specialized interpretations are created that way, yet a drawing, whether of building design or not is for the most part done freehand to deliver the affectability and feeling the craftsman wishes to express. Unadulterated building rendering once in a while display aesthetic enthusiasm!

www.ingramcontent.com/pod-product-compliance
Lightning Source LLC
Chambersburg PA
CBHW080611190526
45169CB00007B/2967